START UP YOUR CHARACTER

Written By: Collin Burdsall

Special Thanks:

Thank you to my wonderful **Parents (Brian and Lois),** brothers **Eric** and **Chris,** and pets. You're all the best. Through good and the bad, we stand together. Nothing can divide the love I have for all of you.

Thank you to **James Mitchell** and your family. You are extraordinary people. You all are family to me. There are people who you meet and never remember again. You all will have a permanent section in my heart.
Jim, you are the reason why I first tried writing. After the completion of my first work, it empowered me to write this book.

Thank you to **Steve**, **Gia**, and the entire Delorie family. This world is so dirty that you can forget that there are good people out. You are proof that great people exist. You are the truest friends I have ever had.

Lastly, thank you to **Bill** "The Professor", **Debby**, and **Greg** Williamson. You are amazing people. Words cannot explain how great you really are.

Table of Contents

Please Read First 7
Refresh Your Mind 10
What They Teach 11
The NECA Philosophy 15
The Streets of Life 17
Your Destination 18
A Map 20
Your Inner Car 26
Broken Down 28
You Have to Want to Change 31
The Engine 33
Negativity 34
   The Fix to Negativity: Open Your
   Options 37

You are What You Think? 40

Self Confidence 42

   The Fix to Self Confidence 45

Your Inner Critic 48

   Shutting Up Your Inner Critic 50

Learn from Others 53

The Tires 56

   Life's Success 57

   Honesty 60

   Does This Make Me Look Fat? 63

   Your Word 66

   Do Something for the Right Reasons 68

Windshield and Windows 73

   The Way to Think of Others 74

   Revenge 76

   Trust 77

The Body 80
Your Look 81
Smile 83
Cleanliness 85
Mirrors 87
The Past 88
Clean Your Mirrors 91
Trial, Error, and Learn 94
Brakes 98
Stop and Relax 99
Slowing Down 102
Breathing 104
Proper breathing 107
Fuel 109
Your Hobbies and Activities 110
Bad Fuels 116

Lights 120
- Emotions 121
- When Emotions Are Up 123
- Up Emotion's Side Effects 125
- When Emotions are Down................. 126
- Down Emotion's Side Effects............. 128
- Solve the Side Effects of Emotions ... 129
- Projecting 132
- The End 134

Please Read First

The biggest hurdle I have to surpass in order to spread my word is my age. There is a belief that someone in their 20's cannot teach somebody anything. These people think that in order to teach someone something, the teacher must have lived it.

Does a history teacher have to live through the 1490's in order to teach their students about Christopher Columbus? Does a Jury have to commit murder in or to sentence a killer? Would it be wrong for a single father to teach his daughter about her gender specific problems during childhood? No!

You are learning every second of your life. Some things could be negative.

Others may be positive. You are going to decide which information you want to filter.

There are plenty of people who are in later stages of age and have no clue how to live a true life. These people do not even attempt to fix the problem. You may know some people like that. The fact that you are giving my book a try proves that you are not one of them.

When you read my book, there is one requirement that I ask. Use your brain. Think about what I write in this book and compare it to your beliefs. If you compare two identical things, neither is better. The only way to find an improvement is to compare something different. Even if you decide to use a portion of ideals in this book, I promise you will be a better person.

Refresh Your Mind

To fully read this book may take a short period of time. This book is specially designed to be read and completed at your own pace. To read the book's material may take hours to read, but can take much longer to master.

Keep this book and read it over at any time. This book is also a reference. It is designed to be read an unlimited amount of times to constantly refresh your mind.

What They Teach

The philosophy that most motivational speakers teach is called Neuro Linguistic Programming. It can also be called Neuro Associative Conditioning. This psychotherapy is considered an alternate treatment. The idea to the philosophy is to deliberately change the emotional and mental behaviors. They oppress what they consider to be a "negative response".

One concept within is to constantly be happy. Never at any point should you be sad in any way. This notion is ridiculous. Could you imagine everyone at a funeral being overjoyed in happiness?

It is natural for you to be sad. It is natural to have emotion. The derivative word to natural is nature.

Animals have emotion. Ask any dog owner and they will agree. When you leave for a prolonged period of time the evidence will be overwhelming. It could be panting, jumping, and barking when you return. It also could be digging, going to the bathroom inside, and/or ripping up the pillows on the couch while you were away. Did you know that antidepressants such as Clomipramine and Fluoxetine are prescribed for dogs with separation anxiety?

Domestic animals are not the only ones that have emotion. Nothing is supposed to be more ruthless then the cold hearted snake. The rattle snake gets his name from the rattle on the end of his tail. The rattle snake shakes his rattle when he is scared and is trying to warn off predators. Wait, did you hear that? Snakes get scared too? That's an emotion!

The rattle at the end of their tail is quite loud. It can be as high as 8,000 hertz (The same as an ambulance siren.) and 75 decibels.

Almost all of the species of rattle snake is venomous. Besides permanent scarring, their venom can cause tissues to be destroyed, blood clotting, and death. Would you want the snake use his rattle, or oppress his emotions and just wait until you are in range to strike?

Neuro Linguistic Programming or any philosophy of its kind is not natural. It is similar to trying to teach a dog to mew and a cat to moo. It can be compared to pharmaceutical medication. If taken incorrectly it can be harmful to you and your loved ones. It's not natural, it's illogical, and it's unhealthy.

The NECA Philosophy

- **N**atural
- **E**lucidative
- **C**onclusive
- **A**cumination

The NECA (Pronounced NEE-KAH) Philosophy is a combination of common sense and problem solving. There is no brain washing and certainly no oppressing of emotions. NECA is natural.

When I say "Natural" this means just that. I am not going to look into a crystal ball to see the future. Nor am I going to tell you to stand on your head and cite the alphabet backwards. The NECA Philosophy is not going to trick you in any way. Since NECA is all natural it can be compared to fruit. You cannot overdose or use it incorrectly.

Part 1: The Streets of Life

Life is like driving down the street. The *street* is the route you take to get to your destination.

Your Destination

Your destination is your goals, dreams, and aspirations. The destination could be the dream job, the book you want to write, the things that you want to see and do before you die, or whatever your heart has yearned. Everyone has a destination. Your destination is waiting for you to arrive.

The difficulty to your destination is not the problem. No matter how hard it may seem for your inner car can get there, it can make it. The problem is the directions.

Without direction, the streets of life are near impossible to get around. There is an endless amount of ways to turn. One wrong turn could lead you into the wrong direction.

A Map

If you try to wing it, getting lost is a definite. The only way you are going to get to your destination is to plan it out. In order to do so, you are going to need a map.

Your *life Map* is going to guide and remind you where you are going. To make a life map, you first need to know where your destination is.

- What is your destination?

Some of us can immediately answer this question without even blinking. These people dream about arriving to their destination. They are what most people call "big dreamers".

Big Dreamers dream about big things. They dream about things like becoming a millionaire, the mayor, and a celebrity. Are these dreams too big? No. Your destination is achievable. No matter how big it may be, if rational, you can make it there.

Some destinations are further apart than others. The harder the difficulty, the further away your destination will be. This does not mean to settle for something easier because of the inconvenience of the distance. This is not going to work. You do not settle for the hardware store because the airport is too far away.

Some people do not know what their destination is. These people are dreaming but are not aware of it. In order to see your dream, you need to really sit back and look into your soul.

What are the things you want to do? You have one guaranteed life. You are living it now. If you do not arrive to your final destination, let it not be from a failure of attempting.

Don't make up a destination just to drive there. You do not have to dream huge. The magnitude of the destination does not matter. The only element to your destination should be the result.

- What is the outcome of your destination?

When you arrive to your destination, does it fill a void? What is this destination accomplishing? Every turn you take on the streets of life needs logic. Without reason, you are doing something for nothing.

- Is the outcome something that completes or begins?

Some dreams are not the finish line to your desires. You may drive to your destination and figure out that it's a *waypoint*.

Goals are miniscule in size compared to your destination. You can accomplish thousands of goals and get no closer to your destination. Someone can make "taking out the trash" a goal to accomplish. This may complete a usual chore, but does not get you any closer towards your dreams.

Waypoints are goals that will advance you forward to your destination. Waypoints will continually lead to other waypoints until you arrive.

- What are the waypoints that are needed in order to arrive to your destination?

You now have a destination with a great reason. Where do you go from here? Now is the time to plan out the route you need to arrive. What are the steps that are needed in order to arrive from where you are? Every destination has requirements.

No matter what your destination is, your first step is always the same. You need to restore your inner car so it can drive again on the streets of life. This is the adventure we are going to go on now.

Your Inner Car

The vehicle that you drive to get to your destination is your character.

When you drive down the street of life in your inner car (Character), traffic (Everyone) can tell everything they need to know about you. Your demeanor is one of many things that people can distinguish by looking at your car.

If you drive down the street in a car that is smashed up, traffic is going to avoid you. This is because of the image that you are portraying. Nobody wants to crash.

To *describe* character properly in a few sentences is impossible. To possess character is plausible. It can be done with discipline. Understanding what is right sometimes is not the easiest to interpret. Those with character do. There is no substitute or shortcut. To attain something so precise, you have to consistently hone its attributes.

To see character is unmistakable. When you are around someone of character, there is no denying it. You either have it or you do not. To acquire character is one of the most prestigious honors that one can have. You are among the elite if you have character.

Broken Down

Have you felt in the past weeks, months, or years that you have not been getting closer to your destination? Does it feel as if nothing is happening in life? Has your life gone to a screeching halt? Have you wanted to get back on the streets of life but cannot seem to get moving anymore?

These symptoms are just a few of your car being *broken down*. It does not matter if it was last year or yesterday; you need to do something right away.

When something breaks in your car, the rest of the car goes with it. It takes only days for your inner car to deteriorate. Your tires are rotted, the engine is blown, it's out of gas, and is sitting in the garage collecting dust.

On the streets of life, you cannot go to a character dealership and get a new car. The car that you have is the car you will drive. When you are broken down there are only two options that you have.

1. Accept that you are stuck. "This is the way it is and there is nothing I can do about it."

2. You can stop dwelling on the problems in your life and concentrate on how to restore your inner car. Turn it from a junker to a Jaguar, a clunker to a Cadillac, or a lemon to a Lamborghini. This will get you back to driving on the streets

and moving towards your destination.

There are two different kinds of people on earth. They are divided into "Movers" and "Sleepers". The choice that you make is going to decide which class that you will fall under.

Sleepers are in the large majority. They will choose path number 1. Sleepers select contentment and mediocrity over a challenge to succeed.

If you choose to become a Mover, then you have chosen path 2. In one choice, you have just opened up a profusion of potential. Movers are within the smallest percentile of people on earth. They are the people who do not take settling for an answer.

You Have to Want to Change

Moving is a big part of the battle of success. Knowing how to correctly move is another. To just move is not enough. To learn how to properly move you have to be willing to change.

I cannot make you change. You are going to be the one that has to *decide* to change. What you have done is your habitual regimen. It is your safe haven.

Your thinking process and philosophies have gotten you where you are today. The only way you are going to get a different outcome from today is to do something differently. Doing the same thing over and over is not going to alter the response.

The only way you are going to restore your inner car is to do it yourself. I am going to give you the resources to do so and tell you how to do it. With this content, I am going to give you the ability to get your car back on the road and driving towards your destination.

What do you say? Let's get building!

Part 2:
The Engine

The engine is the main piece of your car. Without an engine, nothing else will work. Your inner car's engine is *the thinking of yourself.*

Negativity

Negativity is the most common reason for an engine to not work. Negativity is the *act of looking at any scenario in one spectrum.* The spectrum of negativity is the one that is knowingly not the best decision.

Lots of people who are negative try to hide behind the title of "realist" or "pragmatists". These titles refer to the belief of only what is logical.

Being a realist is naïve. Why is succeeding in life not logical? Since when is it fake for good things to happen?

Just because it has not happened, does not make it fake. To put this in proportion, it would be equivalent to saying, "I have never hit a hole in one in golf... So, it has never happened to anyone else." That is silly! With that same logic, if you have never been in space, it is not real either. Ask a NASA astronaut if going into space is fictitious.

The reason why people hide behind words like "realist" is because they don't want to be known as negative. Changing the label on a can of corn to a can of peas is not going to change what is inside.

Even negative people do not want to be known as negative. Why would you?

The Fix to Negativity: Open Your Options

The ideal answer to a problem is the opposite effect. When you want to fix being *bad*, you have to begin to be *good*. When you want to fix doing wrong, you have to begin to do right. When you want no more of the *same*, you have to do things *differently*.

Most people think the opposite of negativity is to be positive. Those people are wrong. As I previously stated, *Negativity is the act of looking at something in one spectrum.*

Positivity is very similar. Positivity is *the act of looking at something in one spectrum.*

Where positivity differs is its focus is on the exultant and unproblematic point of view. Negativity and Positivity are far from the opposite.

It's not the side that you choose that makes it a flawed thinking process. It is the concept as a whole. In order to rid of this nasty habit you need to open your mind. You need to evaluate both aspects at all times. Decide with a non-biased mind which path to choose.

Sometimes the harder path is the one with the superior outcome. This may take a substantial amount of work and have more problems involved, but it's the path that you must take to get the wanted conclusion. If you were in a positive mindset, you would be oblivious to the opportunity. You have to open the box in order to get what's inside. Until you do the contents will remain.

You are What You Think?

The most frequent philosophy that gets tossed around is, "You are what you think". This philosophy sounds too good to be true! That's because it is not true.

The intent of the philosophy was to teach confidence with deceit. Trick yourself into believing a lie. This is another harmful technique that a lot of people teach.

There are mentally ill people that truly believe that they are something that they are not. Whether it's Jesus Crist, a cartoon character, or a farm animal, these people believe it whole-heartedly. With the "You are What You Think" philosophy, these people would be just that. Instead, they are none of the above. They are just crazy.

Never trust a philosophy that can be discredited by the mentally insane. These edgy philosophies are usually incorrect. They try to tell you what you want to hear instead of the truth.

Self Confidence

People are hypercritical of themselves. A large part of it is due to their surroundings. Media has a large influence in how people think and act.

Today more than ever people are connected to each other. Now with the likes of Twitter, Facebook, and other social networking sites the hoi polloi can see what their favorite celebrity is having for breakfast. I am not saying this is a bad thing. This is just another influence in today's society.

When you add in more influences, you add in a proportioned amount of the good and the bad. This tests everyone's decision making on a quantity level. It is up to you to decide which choices are wise.

One extremely popular life decision is plastic surgery. You name the body part; doctors can cut it up and change its appearance. If TV reflected what reality was, everyone would not be able to blink due to facelifts and Botox. Everyone would have huge lips and noses that are too small for our faces.

Nobody gets cosmetic plastic surgery for the physical aspect. They are getting it because of the lack in self-confidence. When a plastic surgeon slices you up, he is not appeasing your body. The doctor is satisfying your mind. Every time someone goes under the knife, they are taking a chance of mutilation or dying. Did I mention that the average cost of plastic surgery is $3634.65 (Before the hospital fees.)?

The Fix to Self Confidence

Self-confidence is a tough task to restore. Some people have bashed themselves so badly they start to believe the insults as facts. These people have set their personal standards so high that it can no longer be ascertainable by anyone.

Self-confidence is the certainty that is inside of you. How confident are you? There is advice that everyone fails to recognize. The scale that rates how good you are at something is not set at the top. The bar is always positioned where you put it.

I hear people say "I am ugly". To whom are you comparing your beauty to? The only mark that you are trying to compete against is your own. The bar should never be put anywhere else.

    You are the most beautiful person that can be compared. You understand everything about yourself. You know more than anyone could ever know about who you are. It does not matter what the cover of a magazine says, beauty is an element in everything. Ugly is the same.

    For anyone to synopsize the entire concept of beauty in the size of one's breasts, lips, nose, or clothing is like saying "the only star in the entire universe is the moon". Not only are you wrong, you are off by an infinite. You are gorgeous in an abundance of ways. Your beauty shines constantly when you are being yourself.

Many of times people refuse to do something because they do not know how. Anyone who uses that as an excuse is being coy. Could you imagine when you were an infant if you had the same thinking? You definitely would not be walking, talking, and you would still be using a diaper.

The answer to a new experience should be "I am going to have to learn". This answer is the most ideal. It takes time and practice to get good at anything. This scenario is universal. It doesn't matter whether you want to become an Olympic gold medalist or want to cook a homemade meal.

Your Inner Critic

You thought of a great idea. Before you could start to work on it, you have already talked yourself out of it! How many times has this happened?

I call this your "inner critic". Your inner critic is going to criticize you. That's the job of an inner critic! If it wasn't doing that, then what else would your inner critic do?

Let's say you are in the mood to go bowling. You have never bowled before. You get ready to go to the bowling alley and then your inner critic appears:

- "You don't know how to bowl!"

- "Why are you wasting your time?"

- "You're going to look stupid."

- "You are going to throw nothing but gutter balls!"

<u>Shutting Up Your Inner Critic</u>

Now it is the time to shut up your inner critic. These things that your inner critic is saying will not bring you down. They will motivate you!

- "You're right! That's why I am going there, to learn."

- "I would rather take my free time bowling and have fun then doing nothing."

- "What does it matter if I look silly? I am a beginner."

- "The more I practice the less gutter balls I am going to throw. If I listen to you, I will never improve."

Let your actions do the quieting. The only way to shut up the inner critic is to prove it wrong. If your inner critic is right once, you are going to start to hear more nagging. Your inner critic will say, "Remember the one time I was right?"

You are not living the life of the inner critic. You are living *your* life. What does it matter if you are not good at it? You will learn and get better over time. The most important thing is that you are experiencing life and *not* experiencing the result of your inner critic.

Learn from Others

When you know about a certain topic, you are more inclined to converse about it. This is your comfort zone of intellect.

Just like any concept in life, confidence can be abused. To know everything about anything is a mere impossible accomplishment. That is due to the world's rapid change every second.

Society is an ever thriving community that adapts to its surroundings. Where it may be acceptable in some areas, it may be frowned upon in others. In order to keep up with society, you have to be constantly aware and willing to absorb information.

People that have the "Know it all" attitude hinder their potential. Their ignorance overshadows their abilities. When you ignore an opportunity to learn information, you are stinting your intellectual growth.

It does not matter if you are in a conversation with someone of lesser knowledge. You should always give someone your undivided attention. When someone is giving you their time, you should be flattered.

Every person you meet is human. They have wants, needs, emotions, and feelings. You have to treat everyone as if they are the most important person in the world.

You need to humble yourself. Understand that a true genius admits when they do not know something. Don't let your pride get the best of you. Instead of pretending to know, be like a sponge and absorb the information.

Everything is learned from another source. It can span from an encyclopedia to television. Provided the information is accurate, the source can be anything.

If you are being taught information you already know, continue listening for possible information you may have forgot or have not learned. Your knowledge is only as limited as you want it to be.

Part 3:
The Tires

The tires on your car grip the street of life and maneuver the car towards your destination. Without tires you are not going anywhere. They also help to avoid obstacles in the future. The tires of your inner car are *trueness*.

Life's Success

When you pass away, the last thing people are going to remember you for is your personal things. When everything comes to an end, physical items that you own will no longer matter. Money will lose its meaning and become colored paper.

The only thing that will carry on is your *legacy*. Some people's legacy will carry on for centuries after their passing. Others will fade away instantly.

While we are alive, we are in a similar situation from death. The stereotypical measurement of success in finances is how much money and equity one acquires in a lifetime.

How do you measure your success as a human? You are offered tons of different variables throughout your lifetime. This is what makes everybody a unique individual.

There is not much a hobo from Cincinnati has in common with a billionaire from Beverly Hills. They are on the opposite ends of the social status. This does not mean that the billionaire is a more successful human then the hobo.

People, who are prosperous in monetary gain, are not guaranteed to be prosperous in their life's level of enjoyment. A hobo may not have lots of money, but can find wealth in other nuances of life.

So, how do we measure the success as a human? The answer is in the trueness of our lives.

Honesty

What is the benefit of telling a lie? Is it the thrill of getting away with it? Maybe it's something that you will acquire. Maybe it's avoiding something that you are embarrassed about?

All of these benefits are transient. They are a temporary gain. Are they worth risking the trust of another? That is the two paths that you are up against:

1. Lie to gain a short result that isn't true.

2. Maintain your integrity and earn an abundance of respect.

The path you should always take is obvious. Never lie about anything. Anytime you are being dishonest, you are driving off of the pavement. You are certain to crash your inner car.

You should challenge yourself to be honest. The bigger the consequence, the more proud you should be when you are telling the truth. Honesty is a tangible that only the finest cars have.

When someone figures out you were not telling the truth, they will no longer trust you the same again. The damage this does to your car is permanent. It does not matter if you never lie again. The person will doubt (Even for a second) what you say for the rest of eternity.

When nobody knows you are lying, there is always one person that does. The person is *you*. This is flattening the tires of your car. In order to become a better person, you need to be better inside and out. Being dishonest is one of the worst things you can do to your car.

Does This Make Me Look Fat?

Your inner car deserves to be recognized as trustworthy. No matter what the degree, you need to remain true. At times it is tough to tell the truth. The hardest seems to be when someone's feelings are at risk.

Everyone knows the stereotypical situation between the couple in the clothing store. The guy is sitting outside of the fitting area while the woman is in there trying on clothing. She walks out and then asks the big question. "Does this make me look fat?"

We know the pickle he is in. What is the guy to do? What if the outfit does make her look fat?" He can't say "The outfit makes you look like a whale!" On the other hand, if he lies, she will buy and walk around in a bad outfit because of his decision.

Do you think there is no right answer? If you said "yes", you are incorrect. There is a way to not hurt someone's feelings and remain true. Instead of saying, "If you were on a farm, the farmer would think you are a cow", try wording the truth so you take another's feelings in consideration. Think about how they will feel if you say something in that manner.

The guy that is in our previous example could easily tell the truth nicely. He could say "That outfit does not do your beauty any justice. I do not know what it is, but it doesn't look right." The two essential elements are:

1. Is it the truth?

2. Is it said in a way that is not insulting, harsh, or mean?

    If they find out that you are lying, the result will be significantly worse. This is damaging your inner car. Never tell a lie, there is no reason to.

Your Word

To be honest throughout our life is a must. It is just as important to stand by your word. When you say you are going to do something, you are putting your word at risk.

You must always be true to your word. This is something that needs no compromising. No matter how frivolous it is to you, others still hear what you are saying. It may not seem so frivolous to them. Your proclamation is an instant test by others to ascertain your reliability.

When you say something, mean it. If what you are saying is a blatant lie, no matter how well you portray it, it will be found out in time. When your word gets a reputation as false, your words will have less meaning than ever.

You deserve to be listened to. You deserve to have your words taken seriously. You owe it to yourself to have your word remain true.

Do Something for the Right Reasons

People do courageous acts. Things that might make you want to do the same. Doing something good is not a problem. Neither is the want to do the same. The problem is when people do good things for recognition. They are not doing it for the right reason.

Think about all of the people that are charitable. How many of them have you seen with the big check? How many times have you seen TV specials that are raising money for a charity?

Recognition and fame are against the spirit of charity. Charity is supposed to be from the heart. It was not intended to try to convince people that you are a good person. Unfortunately, that is the standard of today.

There are two elements in the outcome of your actions. The elements are what you *gain* and *lose*. Gain is what you have received for the choice of actions. Loss is what you could have gained if you would have varied your approach.

For example, a celebrity wants to donate $100,000 dollars to a charity that helps children. He likes how the charity operates and he feels that they can put $100,000 to good use.

He has an event to collect money for this charity. At the end of the fundraiser he has everyone's attention and reveals the big check. The entire audience starts to applause and the audience's main conversation while walking to their car is "Wow, what a great person!"

What did this celebrity gain? Sure he gave a charity $100,000. That could have been accomplished by quietly writing a check. His gain was he received recognition. Everyone walked out of the event talking about how good of a person he is.

What did he lose? Even if the audience knows what the charity is about, this celebrity has taken away from it. If he would have approached the scenario differently, he could have had the people walking away talking about the charity. His loss is the awareness of the charity and the entire spirit of giving.

He chose to be recognized over helping little children. He gave a charity $100,000 dollars for recognition and fame. He gave money for the wrong reason.

The common excuse I hear too often is "I am trying to bring awareness to people". Informing people of anything can be done without recognition or pleading for donations. Inform people of what is going on, then let them decide whether it's worthy of a donation. People do not need you to sacrifice the goodness of your heart for awareness. For all you are trading is virtuousness for selfishness.

The gain and loss concept is not just for giving to charity. It can be applied to any nuance in life. Before you choose to go in a certain direction, be sure that you do it with the right intentions. Make sure you are not losing what you want and gaining something you do not need.

Part 4: Windshield and Windows

The windshield and windows are what help you see traffic. Without them, you will not be able to see where you are driving. The windshield and windows in your inner car are *your perception of others.*

The Way to Think of Others

Too many people see the traffic (Other People) on the streets of life in disgust. They see a fat guy and say, "Why won't he lose weight?" They see a dirty woman and say, "Why doesn't she take a shower?" They see an arrogant guy and say, "Why does he have to act so ignorantly?"

The question I would rather ask is, "Why are you offended?" Another person's weakness is your image's gain. Do not be affronted by ones who are of help.

Instead of seeing the arrogance of the guy 2 spots in front of you at the movie theatre in repugnance, see that person as someone who amplifies your modesty. You should see the dirty women at the grocery store as someone who amplifies your cleanliness. Ugly does an exceptional job of making things beautiful.

Without any bad there would be no good. Good would no longer matter. Without hate there would be no love. Love would no longer exist.

Revenge

When somebody does you wrong, you have to remember that getting revenge is the worst answer. Two wrongs never make a right. Do not drop to the level of the wrongdoer.

Be the better person. You know why they are wrong. For you to do the same, is not going to accomplish anything. Do not become something that you despise. You would then despise yourself.

When you can walk away from a situation and honestly know you did everything to make it right, you should be proud. Getting revenge is something you should never be proud about.

Trust

Trust is something that is a must. No matter how hard you try, you will have to trust others. If you order something from the internet you are trusting lots of people to get the product to your doorstep.

- You trust everyone that made the computer. If it does not work, the order would not be possible.

- The company that makes the product you ordered and their entire staff

- The workers at the warehouse to get the product ready to ship

- The shipping company that delivers it to your state and county

- The delivery guy who puts the product to your doorstep

This is a vague example of the amount of trust that is needed for something as secluded as ordering a product off of the internet. Trusting in people is something that you need to embrace.

I am not saying go to a crime ridden place in your local area and walk around with lots of money in your hand. Nor am I saying to mortgage your home to send money to scam artists and trust they will come through.

What I am saying is don't think that the whole world is out to get you. You need to put your fears behind and enjoy life to the fullest. The world is a beautiful place. Unless you start trusting more and put down your guard at times, you will never be comfortable enough to enjoy what the world has to offer.

Part 5:
The Body

The body of the car is what covers everything. It has lots of safety values. It also encases the engine, holds the windows in place, and is the main focus in appearance.

Your inner car's body is *your physical appearance.* What do people see when you drive your car down the street? Is this the reaction that you want?

Your Look

First impressions stay for a lengthy duration. Other's impressions of you will be made within the first 20 seconds. There are lots of scenarios that require great first impressions.

Spanning from acing the big job interview or trying to impress a future love interest, your appearance is going to set the tone for what's next to come. I am not saying go to the gym and get a six pack of abs. I am talking about little subtleties that will portray the look you are going for.

Smile

The smile is definitely underused. A smile can change a person's day dramatically. I love to go to public places and smile at the people I pass. You can witness what it looks like to see a human lighten up.

How many times have you made a poor decision in a bad mood? In retrospect, would you of reacted differently if you were in a better mood? The mood you are in is a huge factor in the choices you make.

Your smile could be the difference between the recipient making a rash decision and one that is done in an uplifting state of mind. Something as insignificant as a smile can dramatically alter another's life.

You need to make it a habit to smile at others. Before you walk into a place remember to smile and do it often. Make it an appoint to walk where there is people and try it out.

Cleanliness

The last thing you want to do is drive around in a dirty car. Traffic's first impression will surely be a negative one. Not only is it unhealthy, it lets everyone know that you cannot handle your own hygiene.

You need to stay clean. Your daily regimen should be:

- Bathing
- Brushing your hair and teeth
- Deodorant
- Keeping your hair trimmed (Head and body)

A clean look does not stop at just your daily regimen. Your apparel and accessories need to be clean too. Wearing a dirty shirt is a huge blow to your character.

You are going to decide what world you are going to live in. Ugly people live in an ugly world. Do you want to live in an ugly world? If so, then become an ugly person. Bad people live in a bad world. Dirty people live in a dirty world. Polar bears live in the snow. That's why polar bears are white.

Part 6:
Mirrors

Think of mirrors as reflective windows. Mirrors let you know what is coming up from behind you. Mirrors also inform you what is beside you so you do not crash into fellow traffic. Without mirrors on everyone's cars, the road would be impossible to drive on.

The mirrors in your inner car are the *past*. Your mirrors display the things that you have driven by. You cannot drive safely down the street of life without mirrors.

The Past

On the streets of life there are two directions you can drive.

1. Away from you destination (Past)
2. Towards your destination (Future)

The route that you want to take is the one that is always geared towards your destination. The road that you have already driven by is behind you and gone. You cannot arrive to your destination driving in the wrong direction.

The mirrors on your inner car are not for staring. When you start to stare at the mirrors, you are taking your eyes off of the road ahead. On the streets of life anything can happen at any time. You need to be focused on the pavement ahead to avoid any obstacles.

It is too common for people find a smooth road and decide to not leave.

They find complacency so they don't drive any further. They don't want to drive any closer to their destination in fear that the next road is going to be bumpier.

When you drive, you are going to hit bumps. You are going to have obstacles in life that weren't there on the road before. If you want to really get to your destination, you will have to drive over some bumps in the road. The bump will be past you and in your mirror after you drive over them.

Clean Your Mirrors

In very dramatic times, it can be hard to let go of what has happened. When you drive, your mirrors will get dirty. This is especially true when you have driven for an extensive period of time. The dirt on your inner car's mirrors are the bad times of the past.

If your mirrors become partially dirty, you cannot drive with the same confidence you once did. You cannot make the same choices. Confidence is pivotal when you need to make big decisions.

When your mirrors get so dirty that they are no longer functional, you cannot make any rational decisions of any degree.

You are now guessing. The next choice could be the one that crashes your car.

You should check for dirt on your mirrors before you drive. As soon as you see any dirt on your mirrors, you need to clean them off before they become unusable. You cannot afford any type of obstruction of any sort. Your safety is the most essential part of driving down the road.

You cannot clean your mirrors while you are operating your vehicle. Once your car is safely parked, now is the time to clean your mirrors. The best solution to cleaning your past is the present.

Wipe away the dirt with a new perspective. *Your present is what will be in your mirror next.* If your past never was, what is the product of today? Look in the mirrors and know that no matter how ugly it looks, it can be changed. If yesterday is ugly today, it will make tomorrow's yesterday look that much better.

Trial, Error, and Learn

Nobody can change what has already been done. Too many times people look at a bad part in their lives and dwell on the negative aspect of the situation. They get stuck in a pity party and forget to learn.

Horrible moments in your life should not be looked at negatively. You should be thankful that these events have happened and are behind you. These events (No matter the degree of atrocity.) were "Life Teachers". They taught you a valuable lesson in what is wrong. The lesson is what you should bring with you, not the unpleasantness.

Consequences are among the top of human's biggest fears. If you knew you couldn't be harmed, would you walk through a burning building? Why not? Imagine you are a high roller at a game of poker. Every dollar you lose magically replenishes. Would you be afraid to call someone's bluff? Nobody would be afraid. Why not put it all-in every hand?

You won't walk into a burning building because you can be severely burnt or die. You won't put your money all-in every hand because you could lose it. These are the consequences that supply your reaction.

When the conclusion to the responsibility is fantastic, there is a line of traffic waiting to take claim. On the contrary, taking responsibility for your actions when the outcome is bad is what only the greatest cars do.

The three essential parts to accepting your consequences is trial, error, and learn. *Trial* is the act of understanding what the situation is all about. In the engine section I talked about opening your options and looking at all of them completely. Trial is examining each option *after* you have made your decision.

Error is determined after you see the conclusion. Was it the wrong path? Could I have altered it in some way? Was there a different path to take?

Learning is the most important part of all. Once you decide if the path was appropriate, learn why the incorrect choice is wrong. The common belief is to learn what is right. This is a tedious task. There is only one right answer. When you focus on what is wrong, you can analyze a vast amount of lessons in one problem.

Part 7: Brakes

The brakes are what help you slow down and stop your vehicle. On the streets of life, getting to your destination is not about never stopping. Life is about continuing forward after every time you stop. The brakes on your inner car are *relaxation*.

Stop and Relax

Stopping is healthy. You need to be able to sit back and take it easy. Set a time during the day that would be most convenient and relax for at least 30 minutes. This could also be split up in multiple sessions as well. For example, you could have three 10 minute sessions.

You need to plan on when your session will be. You do not want to stop on an impulse. If you decide to stop all at once you are going to squeal your tires, lose control, and possibly fly through the windshield.

For the first week, your sessions should not have any type of stimulation. This includes TV, music, hobbies, and so on. This is to see if exiling your mind is the superior form of relaxation.

After a week has past, you now can use your relaxing sessions with stimulants. Do what is most relaxing to you. It could be a hobby all alone or watching TV with your friends or loved ones.

If for any reason the things you are doing during your relaxing session do not relax you, return to your exile relaxing sessions. You can keep experimenting with activities later. The most important thing to do while you are at your sessions is to relax.

Driving down the street as fast as you can and never stopping is a disaster waiting to happen. Everybody stops at one point or another along their travels. Don't let your car crash due to pride or impatience.

Slowing Down

The brakes are not just for going to a complete stop. Another function to your brakes is to reduce speed. This is a great way to slow your car down from going too fast and continue moving forward.

Everybody can relate to speeding at one time or another. You get extremely focused on what is ahead of you, when you look down, you are going too fast. What can you say? Life can sneak up on you.

Slowing down can be performed by gently pressing the brakes. This will not stop the car's movement but will reduce your speed so you can continue moving forward safely.

To gently press your breaks in your inner car, you need to learn to breathe properly.

Breathing

I know what you are thinking. I breathe automatically. If I didn't know how to breathe, then I wouldn't be alive. Believe it or not, most people have taught themselves to breathe incorrectly.

When your body is under a great deal of tension, you start to compensate your normal breathing patterns with very short holds of your breathe. The holding of the air is so customary that you cannot detect that you are doing it.

When stress arrives, improper breathing starts to take place. When you breathe incorrectly you are not giving your body enough oxygen and too much carbon dioxide. The side effects of not enough oxygen are:

- Having aches in the body
- Becoming Anxious
- Having a mental block
- Feeling dizzy or nauseas
- Extremities can have slight numbness
- Chest pain
- Problems digesting

Breathing improperly can be easily cured. When you feel that your car is driving too fast down the streets of life, you need to slow it down. To slow it down you need to deep breathe.

When you start to feel some stress, take your focus off of the road for just a second and look at the speedometer. How fast am I going?

To decide your current speed, think about what you normally do on a stress free day. Then, think about what is the most stressful situation in the past week. Only seven days, that's it.

Now, think of 1 being a stress free day, and 10 being your week's most stressful. From a range from 1 to 10, how is your current situation (1 being the lowest stress level and 10 being the highest.)? If you said any number over 3, then stop and take some deep breaths. Here is how to do so properly:

Proper breathing

- First you need to take a deep breathe expanding your abdominal area and through your nose until your lungs are full of air.

- Hold the air in your lungs for 3 seconds while you count inside of your head slowly "1, 2, *and* 3."

- Then slowly exhale out of your mouth. Collapsing your abdominal area.

Repeat this exercise three consecutive times. This will slow your inner car down and have you returned to your normal breathing pattern. Besides, do you really want to get a ticket for speeding?

Part 8:
Fuel

Fuel is what keeps your car moving. Without it your car would be immobilized. When your tank is running low, you need to stop at a station and fuel up.

Your car's fuel is your hobbies and activities outside of your destination. They are the things you enjoy doing when you are not driving on the streets of life.

Your Hobbies and Activities

Focusing on the streets of life is very important. Continuing forward is crucial but not a constant. You need to stop and refuel when your tank is low. If you do not refuel, you are going to burn out.

Some people can name the hobbies they enjoy right off top of their head. Others cannot name a single one. Does this mean that you have no hobbies? NO!

A hobby is defined as an activity engaged in for pleasure and relaxation during spare time. If during your spare time you like to peel bananas and duct tape the peels to the walls of your bedroom in the shape of a heart, as strange as this might seem, this is a hobby.

If you want to find some new hobbies, it's quite simply. Think about the things you do every day. What do you enjoy doing? What are the highlights to your average day? Your hobbies are sometimes so subtle that you do not realize it.

Do you really enjoy a good meal? Why not make a hobby out of cooking recipes? That is one that everyone can enjoy. There are unlimited resources to further your hobby. For instance, you can find recipes:

- On TV (they even have specific channels)
- On the internet
- Cook books
- On some of the labels on the food products at the store

Do you have a camera? Why not capture photography? Go around your surrounding and capture photography that you can keep for a lifetime.

You can even take a hobby with a camera further, why not Scrapbook? Take all of your photos and make beautiful books out of them to cherish in the future.

Do you enjoy a quiet day of relaxation? Instead of doing it on the couch, why not take it to a park bench at a nice area close by? You will get some fresh air and enjoy the world's continual movement.

Do you have a favorite show or sport on TV? Why not find a forum that has people that have the same interests? It's not limited to Television; there is a forum for just about anything. If there isn't a forum for what you like, why not make one?

How about gardening? You do not need a yard to do it. Buy a pot and some seeds. Research how to take care of the seeds in order for it to grow into a beautiful plant. The instructions are usually on the seed's packet. If not the case, surely the internet and books will have the info.

Find fun little hobbies that you just enjoy doing. They could be from collecting to learning something new. If you want to donate some of your time, there are lots of places that are in need of a helping hand.

If you do decide to donate your time, don't forget the Part in this book on

"Tires". Donate your time for the right reasons. Your gain is to help others, not receive praise.

When your tank is full again, get back on the road and continue forward towards your destination. The guidelines to hobbies are:

- They must be enjoyed
- It must **NOT** be a bad fuel

Bad Fuels

Never put bad fuels in your engine. Bad fuels are ones that are:

- Unethical
- Illegal
- Harmful
- Going to make you or others feel bad
- Something you will not enjoy

Illegal drugs and alcohol are a primary example to bad fuels. Not only is it unethical and illegal, it is going to harm your body. The feeling of being drunk that people and media glamourize, is nothing more than the feeling you get when you dehydrate your brain and harm your organs.

People use alcohol to hide behind being "Drunk". This is a device so they can get away with making improper decisions. The media has made it "cool". They tell you to drink so much that your body will give up and finally you pass out on the floor.

Do you think that the alcohol companies tell you this because they are concerned about how cool you are? Do you think that drinking until you pass out is advice that is trying to help? No. The reason they say this is because they want you to drink as much of their product as possible. It is a marketing ploy to make huge profits.

Take a week of your time and see if you can count how many times you see alcohol being glamourized. Whether it's from the beautiful models that magically appear when you open a can, to the TV show that features the hip frat boys having a drinking contest.

If you are on illegal drugs, cigarettes, or alcohol you should properly stop using them as soon as possible. These bad fuels are ruining your inner car from the inside. They are ruining your life.

Don't fall for peer pressure. If someone near you in traffic is speeding don't do the same. That is their ticket and not yours. No matter how much of your surrounding say otherwise, you are *ALWAYS* responsible for your actions.

If somebody thinks badly of you because you won't bend to their influence, that's fine let them go their own direction. These people are not your friends at all. They are not worth your friendship. There are about 7 billion people on earth. If several do not like you, there is still well over 6 billion to fall back on.

Part 9:
Lights

There are a plethora of lights on a car. Each light has a function. The headlights illuminate the road in front of you when it is dark. The check engine light informs you when there is something wrong with the engine. Your inner car's lights are your emotions.

Emotions

Everybody is constantly going through emotions. Dealing with our emotions is a tough task. When something very stimulating occurs, it becomes even more difficult.

A lot of times your emotions can get the best of you. You say things in the heat of the moment that you wouldn't of if you weren't so full of emotion. As you know from the "Mirrors" part in this book, you cannot rewind the past and make it right. You should restrain yourself from making big decisions while you are very emotional.

All emotions can be labeled into one of two categories. The categories are *Up* and *Down*. The next time you start to feel emotional you need to classify which category your current emotional state falls under.

When Emotions Are Up

When your emotions are up, a lot of times you can lose control of what you are trying to do. Up emotions are ones that are elevated from your normal state. Here is a list of some UP emotions:

- Awe
- Curiosity
- Euphoria
- Gratitude
- Happiness
- Hope
- Interest
- Joy
- Love
- Lust
- Surprise
- Wonder

Up Emotion's Side Effects

Up emotions are natural. The problem is not the emotion. The problem is the emotion's side effect.

When you are feeling up, what are the problems that you occur? No matter the severity, write down on a piece of paper all of the side effects that occur when you experience Up emotions.

Read through them once more. Add any more side effects that you may have left out. Feel free to update this list at any time.

When Emotions are Down

When your emotions are down you can very easily lose control. Downed emotions are ones that depress your normal state. Here is a list of some downed emotions:

- Anger
- Annoyance
- Disappointment
- Envy
- Embarrassment
- Fear
- Frustration
- Grief
- Guilt
- Hatred

- Horror
- Hysteria
- Jealousy
- Misery
- Pity
- Regret
- Remorse
- Worry
- Suffering
- Sorrow
- Shame
- Depression
- Sadness

Down Emotion's Side Effects

Down emotions are natural. The problem is not the emotion. The problem is the emotion's side effect.

When you are feeling down, what are the problems that you occur? No matter the severity, write down on a piece of paper all of the side effects that occur when you experience down emotions.

Read through them once more. Add any more side effects that you may have left out. Feel free to update this list at any time.

Solve the Side Effects of Emotions

You now have lists of side effects written down. These lists will be your guide to help cure the side effects of both up and down emotions.

Whenever you start to feel emotional, identify whether it is an up or down emotion. After identification, you will say inside of your head, "I will not _____ ". The blank is the ENTIRE corresponding list to your up or down side effect. Here's an example.

Every time Willy gets *angry* he starts to break things around the house. So, he identifies that anger is a downed emotion and he writes this side effect under the "Downed Side Effect List".

Willy has another side effect. When he is sad he throws away valuable things and later regrets it. Once again, Willy identifies and writes it down under the "Downed Side Effect List".

Lastly, every time Willy gets excited he starts to talk really loud. Willy identifies that being excited is an "Up" emotion and writes that on the "Up Side Effect List".

The next time something angers Willy. He will go to his "Down Side Effect List" and say in his head. "I will not break things in the house. I will not throw away anything of value."

Notice that when you read your list, it does not matter what the specific emotion is. When you are feeling any downed emotion, you will read the *ENTIRE* downed list in your head.

The biggest problem is when someone gets emotional they are no longer in their normal state. They do not know what to do in their new emotional state and fill the voids with unwanted reactions. These lists will rid of all of the unwanted things to avoid. By doing this, it will make it easier to find out what to do. A good way to find something is to know where it is not.

Projecting

In order for you to safely drive down the street, you need to use all of your lights properly. You do not want to use your left turn signal and turn right. Not only is that silly, it is also a safety hazard.

An even bigger mistake that people make is they do not use their light at all. You need to project your lights brightly and consistently. They need to be seen by others in traffic. For example, when you need to get away and relax you need to show it. Use your brake lights to show traffic that you are stopping. By doing this you are preventing traffic from crashing into you.

Don't be afraid of making yourself readable. This is the way to let everyone know how you are feeling. When you hold your emotions in, the next time you use them they will come out in concentration. You do not want to have your brake lights blinding traffic. This will cause a crash.

Project your lights brightly and consistently. Imagine if someone replaced their headlight bulbs with the bulbs from Christmas lights. These lights would not be bright enough. Whether it's up or down, you need to project your emotions minus the side effects.

The End

To have a truly superior car, you must do extraordinary things. You control where your car gets to. When you restore your car and get it back on the streets of life, be sure to honk the horn at me as we both make our way to our destination.

                                        Have a safe drive!
                                        Collin Burdsall

NOTES

NOTES

NOTES

NOTES

NOTES

www.ingramcontent.com/pod-product-compliance
Lightning Source LLC
Chambersburg PA
CBHW061443040426
42450CB00007B/1183